MAN VS. NATURE

CONTROLLING FOREST FIRES

NATURE BOOKS FOR KIDS

Children's Nature Books

BABY PROFESSOR

EDUCATION KIDS

Speedy Publishing LLC
40 E. Main St. #1156
Newark, DE 19711
www.speedypublishing.com

Forest fires can start for many reasons. But once they get going, they can burn both forests and homes until they go out or are put out. Read on and find out how to control forest fires.

Forest fire.

HOW FOREST FIRES START

Fires of any kind, from the cozy blaze in fireplace to a huge fire burning through hundreds of acres of forest, need three things: *Heat, Oxygen,* and *Fuel.*

A fire starts from a source of *Heat.* Lightning can strike a tree, or a person can drop a match, but there is always heat at the start of a fire. How much heat the fire needs to get going depends on the next two elements.

Lightning strike to a tree.

What a forest fire burns, the *Fuel* includes dry grass, leaves and pine needles on the ground, trees that have died and fallen, and similar material. If the fire finds enough fuel that is dry and ready to burn, it will catch and grow quickly. Once it has become large and fierce, the fire can threaten living trees, even though green wood resists burning.

A fallen tree is burned to the ground.

The fire needs *Oxygen.* When it is small and just starting, a puff of wind can put the fire out again. But once a fire is under way, a strong wind can be the fire's ally. It brings more oxygen to where the fire is using it, and carries sparks and embers downwind in search of even more fuel.

Raging fire in a forest fire.

Wildfire close up at day time.

HOW TO STOP A FOREST FIRE

If you can cut off one of the three essentials, the fire will stop. It is pretty hard to stop air, and therefore oxygen, from getting to a forest fire, and once the fire is under way it provides its own heat that keeps it going. So most of the time we try to deprive the fire of more fuel. Once it uses up the fuel it can get to, the fire will die.

Here are some ways to cut off the fire from new fuel:

DANGER

BACK 159M / 500r-T

FIRELINES AND FIREBREAKS

When it is clear what direction a fire is moving in, or if there are homes or other vulnerable areas to protect, firefighters often clear a strip of land of anything a fire can burn. They may use bulldozers to plow under trees, underbrush, and dry grass; they may spray fire retardant to make what lies there less burnable, as well as dousing the area with water.

Brush Fire.

If they can, firefighters extend the fireline completely around the fire, to cut it off from more fuel even if the wind changes direction. Then they can let the fire burn itself out.

Fire coals during a firefighting operation.

CONTROLLED BURN

To make a fireline quickly, firefighters may start a small, controllable fire to burn up the fuel in a wide strip before the forest fire can get to it. They may burn along one side of a road so that the width of the road and the width of the already-burned area may stop the fire from extending in that direction.

One danger of doing controlled burns is that, if the conditions are right (dry and windy), the "controlled" fire can get out of control. Now you have two forest fires, instead of one.

Fire starter.

WATER BOMBERS

For large forest fires, the team fighting the fire may call in special planes that can carry a cargo of water and fire-retarding chemical on the fire, or just ahead of the fire. The idea, again, is to reduce the amount of fuel the fire can use.

The water bombers often have ammonium phosphate mixed into their cargo of water, as it further reduces how burnable things are. Water bombers can drop thousands of gallons at a time, but for a large fire that may not have much effect.

Water bomber puts out a wild fire.

HI-TECH TRACKING

Firefighters now can rely on satellite images, computer modelling of what the fire is likely to do, up-to-date weather forecasts, and accurate information about wind direction. This helps them know which way the fire is likely to go next, and helps them work to stop the fire without putting themselves in danger.

Forest after fire.

AL
FIRE

WELL-EQUIPPED FIREFIGHTERS

To fight a forest fire well, the team needs good equipment and training. They wear oxygen masks because the fire is using the oxygen near it; they wear fireproof clothing to keep safe if the fire suddenly changes direction. Firefighters often carry emergency fireproof shelters they can lie under if they become trapped by the fire. The shelters reflect the heat of the fire and will not burn themselves, so a firefighter can shelter under one until the edge of the forest fire moves on.

Forest fire fighters.

Raging Wildfire.

GETTING AHEAD OF FOREST FIRES

It's important to remember that all forests have fires, and that the rhythm of the life of a forest depends on periodic fires to clean out dead material, replenish the soil, and make way for new growth. The problem is when a fire threatens homes, or burns down so many acres of forest that it takes away habitat animals rely on.

It's also important to remember that not all areas need the same approach to keep the risk and damage of forest fires to a minimum. For example, in Northern California, forest management involves annual controlled burns of parts of the forests to remove dead, dry wood and other fuel without letting the fire get out of hand.

Closeup of flaming stump.

On the other hand, the hills of Southern California are covered with oily, flammable underbrush like chapparal. Using controlled burns in this type of environment does nothing to reduce large forest fires, because if you burn the chapparal it is just replaced with other, equally-flammable grasses and bushes. The techniques that work in the tall forests in the north of the state are not only incorrect, but actually harmful, in the different environment in the south of the state.

Aerial view of a veld fire.

DEFEND YOUR SPACE

When forest fires rage, a lot of homes may burn. But most of those homes are not near the actual fire. They burn because cinders and sparks from the fire blow down-wind, and find suitable fuel, like dead leaves in the gutter of a house. The cinders or sparks that find fuel, and have access to oxygen, can start a new fire as much as a mile from the parent forest fire.

Burning grass in the field.

Living trees and bushes resist burning, but dead leaves that have not been raked up, pine needles, and similar fuel are an easy location in which a new fire can start.

Southern California has a particularly dangerous period each year when dry weather and high winds can send sparks and embers flying long distances ahead of forest fires. Experts recommend that people living in the area do a fall clean-up of their properties, getting rid of dryer lint, pine needles, stacks of dry scrap wood and other material that would welcome a spark.

Forest fire.

Forest Fire.

PREVENTING FOREST FIRES

You may not be a firefighter, but you can take steps to keep forest fires from starting!

KEEP YOUR AREA CLEAR OF FUEL

If you live in a dry area where fires are likely, make sure you have removed any piles of pine needles and dry leaves from around your house.

PAY ATTENTION

If you are thinking about having a picnic in the woods, or going camping overnight, have you checked what the danger level is for forest fires? If the level is high, you should not start a fire, even to cook a marshmallow!

Big walpurgis night fire.

DON'T START LITTLE FIRES ON YOUR PROPERTY

It may be tempting to burn that big pile of leaves and branches after you have raked it up, rather than putting it in bags to take to the composting center. But you may start a fire that spreads, catching the grass beside the leaf pile or even branches of nearby trees!

Even though you can't see flames, the fire may be working its way along the root systems of trees and shrubs under your lawn, looking for a place where it can emerge and get going where nobody is paying attention.

PREPARE THE SITE

If you are going to have a fire outdoors, make a wide circle of cleared ground. Keep the supply of firewood you want to use later safely away from the fire as it burns right now. If you don't, you may suddenly find you have a much larger fire than you wanted.

Around the campfire

STAY WITH THE FIRE

If you started a fire, stay with it until it's out. Even if you don't see leaping flames, that does not mean the fire has cooled down and could not blaze up again.

Young couple camping

MAKE SURE THE FIRE IS REALLY OUT

When you are done with the fire, spread any remaining fuel apart, then drown the whole fire with water. Then use a shovel to turn the ashes, and drown it again. You may have to repeat this several times until the fire is safely out.

Don't bury the fire: that may just let it work along through root systems until it is far from where you are paying attention.

Night long exposure photograph of the Santa Clarita wildfire

AN EXCITING PLANET

Fire is a good and useful thing. Fire out of control can be dangerous and destructive. Any element of our wonderful Earth can be dangerous to us if there is too much of it! Read other Baby Professor books, like *Ocean Tides and Tsunamis and Dangerous Weather Phenomena to Look Out For*, to learn more about such dangers.

Visit
BABY PROFESSOR
EDUCATION KIDS
www.BabyProfessorBooks.com
to download Free Baby Professor eBooks
and view our catalog of new and exciting
Children's Books